5 out of 5 per

Copyright © 2021

ISBN: 9798726028125

FOREWORD

This poetry collection is MY story. It has been my outlet for the past 18 months of what we nowadays brand abuse 'recovery'. I am immensely proud of how emotionally far I have come, and with those around me who helped me. In reality, mental illness is an everlasting beast which never truly goes away. Day by day we just learn to cope that little bit better. This is by surviving.

Each poetry collective represents an entirely different aspect of recovery. The first one being each emotion that I experienced or suppressed throughout my initial abuse recovery combined with a dedication to my late nan. However, there is a single message I attempt to portray; that we CAN outgrow our mental illness. We CAN move forward - however long it takes, however many little steps are needed and however much support we need to ask for along the way!

Recovery Is A Journey, Different For All.

This is an image of my first tattoo which I designed myself. It has great meaning to me and always will. It is a symbol of my overall healing process! - (currently three years since my first assault).

5 OUT OF 5

1.0

DEAR NAN:

A COLLECTION OF MY EMOTIONS;

Disclaimer - The images in this section are all photogrpahs of paintings completed by my late nan. They may appear similar to other paintings but are however all illustrated by Elaine Revell and are in no way intended to impersonate any other artist.

An Introduction To Emotion;

Love In Venice

Pound after pound
Break after break
Lie after lie
Lesson after lesson

She wandered, empty streets
Who could have guessed;
The pain she felt;
Enclosed

There was no such 'quick fix',
There was no such 'sweet treat',
There was only deep-rooted fear
There was only small-minded men

But she knew her worth in gold;
And so she kept on roaming
The blank pavement extending
She learnt to love herself

She learnt to LOVE herself;
In Venice

Curious In Bloom

Curiosity killed the cat, she said
Intertwining with the transparent greenery
A mind mangled with extraneous thoughts
A heart tangled with the intensity

Curiosity killed the cat, she said
Applying a dainty feminine touch
A body tired with emotional distress
A hand fired with oppressed passion

Curiosity killed the cat, she said
Solving natures most pressing bunches
A mind mangled with extraneous thoughts
A heart tangled with the intensity

Heartbreak Apartment

Falling
From 12 feet up
A sheer drop
A heart already shattered

Splintered
The cracks on the bannister
From top to bottom
I am broken simultaneously

Abandoned
Failing to attempt resurrection
Some things cannot be; 'fixed'
Some things remain; 'unable'

Empty
The worst of all
Loss is power,
To those who do not lose

Private Peace

Through the pines, into the blur of green,
Within the sea of (near) silence,
During natures year long call,
Do I find my private peace

Through the pines, into the blur of green,
Within the ever-masked beauty,
During the earth's monthly orbit,
Do I find my private peace

Through the pines, into the blur of green,
Within the omnipotent oak breeze,
During MY time,
Do I find my private peace

Crystal Fantasy

And what extra-ordinary construct of society did
you dream up tonight, young girl?

Only the freedom of humanity from the tight chains of
mental illness;
I whispered

Only the prosper of confidence from the spite of those with
small minds;
I whispered

Only the subtle peace of mind from the dark acts of evil;
I whispered

Only the sight of adoration from the guarded love we
idolise;
I whispered

Only the care of words from the ignorant tabloid press;
I whispered

Not a lot sir, not a lot...

Overwhelmed In Nature

It's a wonderful thing, substantial surprise
For it entices the body into attention

The adrenaline rush lights up your eyes
When it splices into your system

There are not many things just as pure
For it takes over, a magical spell
Your imagination sprints wild throughout
Then, you succeed, excel

Windy roots expand and respire
They nurture, eat and pray
But most prominently they later expire
- they grow overwhelmed in May

2.0

SHE BELIEVED
SHE COULD:

SO SHE DID;

An Introduction To Mental Health Recovery;

Two Broken Halves

Glancing accross the surface
You may see one broken soul
A single ounce of might
Nothing filling the hole

As time goes on
All but nothing is left
Seen trembling at this feat
She drowns, a victim of theft

A daily battle consumes her
One step forward yet two steps back
A never-ending cycle
Each time she is bound to crack

But, take a breath
She is still here
A soldier none the less
Recovery is near

And Then I Found You

I was stuck, black holes sprawling
Dreaming daily nightmares
I was messy, crawling
And then I found you

I got off my feet
I took the first steps
I looked into the future
And then I found you

I saw with my eyes
The hurt I had taken
Absorbed, believed, mistaken

I saw with my eyes
The new gift I was given
Enlightened, distinguished, smitten

Forever is a promise
And you made me two
To love and to cherish
Through old and through new

I love that; I found you

Butterfly

Lend a hand to nature
Caress your own heart
It wont break you
At least not apart

To put yourself at ease
You need to let go
You need to forget
You NEED to say no

Breathe in for four
Hold to seven
Exhale to eight
Repeat to eleven

If only it was magic...
Because then maybe
Just maybe;
This world wouldn't be so evidently tragic?

But reality forms
Just as life does
And we snap back to 'normal'
And we re-think our 'choices'

We are bound to human precedent
Morality and belief
For god sake
What a relief.

I Simply Give You Permission

I simply give you permission
To not be 'okay'
To not be 'perfect'
To not be based on standard

I simply give you permission
Which you can in time give yourself
If you simply fight by ignoring
Focus on the height you are soaring

Anywhere with your heart x

At Fourteen

Jump
That's what you're telling me to do?
You trampled carelessly over me
After ALL you put me through

My body feels like it's yours
After you pinned me straight down
I begged you 'another day'
Carrying on, you took me 'a clown'

You told me it was all a joke
That I had said 'no'
You pushed me around
I waited everyday for you to go

When we finally stepped outside
The snow was crisp and falling
Ignorant to the previous events
Your father was calling

I remember the pyjamas,
The blue I was wearing
When you chose to take from me
An impurity I can never resolve
My tainted virginity,
I can never get back

You branded me 'dirty'
After all you had done
Filled with anger
Broken, I have become

I can see the train coming
I am stood on the bridge
I wait here praying
Is there hope? A smidge

You're a silly little boy
And my life is worth more
I am not just a toy,
Keep the shorts you tore

A New Journey

The high and the low
The blue ocean flow
As the tide fluxuates;
I ride the wave of recovery

Self love, Self hate
All that lies inbetween
A different location
A new found identity

You cannot heal surrounded,
By the environment that once broke you
Piece by aching piece
A half becomes a whole

3.0

JUSTICE ON
A PLATE

Justice On A Plate - A Narrative Poem

You may not have been held accountable in court
You may never contact me again
You may not have been 'criminally fought'
But you will ALWAYS be to blame

Justice is served,
On a piping hot plate
You are an imposter
Never a clean slate

My justice is living
She is me, not you
A journey to hell and back
What you put me through

...

You do not deserve your freedom
Nor to perform on life's stage
You should be where you left me,
A pitiful, broken cage

You tried to burden me
You didn't stop poking
Your 'gift' - a life sentence
You harassed me till choking

A magician of sorts
You chase after me
In front of them, nice
I wonder who you might be

...

A spiritless man
Your desire lies false
Seen, you run away

A careless man
Your mind ill natured
Seen, you run away

A possessive man
You attempt ownership
Seen, you run away

...

I will never forgive you
And neither will the rest
That is my justice
Put it to the test

Face what you did
Take a big bow
I dare you to try
I am much stronger now

Justice is served,
She is me

MISS AIMEE LOUISE REVELL

- This narrative poem is aimed at all the attackers and abusers I have once faced. It conveys a single message - you have not broken me, nor will you ever break me.

There are many victims of sexual abuse that choose for good reason not to report their assault, or do report it and it unfortunately makes no progress. They deserve just as much respect and support. Justice may be 'out of reach' for some of us, however being at peace within ourselves serves just as much purpose.

They cannot ruin our lives, we will fight and we will one day be happy again. They will not win. I admire every single one of you who are living and fighting every single day.

4.0

ONE FEMALE
TOO MANY

An Introduction To Sexual Abuse Survival;

Spiral

The image lives hostage in my mind,
Of you and everything you have done
Crouching, alone in this room
Another nightmare has begun

I toss and I turn
My thoughts riddled with fear
Your body sleeps far away
But your presence is right here

Come morning the sun shines
'It wasn't real' I repeatedly say
But my body is still trembling
Will this ever go away?

A... What?

Taken
My future; your promise

Who are you?

Abuser
Attacker
A friend?

A secret?

A secret hiding
In the grey matter
At the very back of my circling mind

Round and round
You come and you go
I can process the sound
I said no.

Still Not Asking For It.

Still not asking for it.
We are not the problem
Your desires are ruthless
You crave control

Still not asking for it.
We are not the problem
Your actions are violent
You abuse her

Rapist.

I will name you for what you are, for what you have done.
Why is it you are so willing to chant discrimination?
So willing to 'make' her yours,
Yet you won't own your identity?

Still not asking for it.
You are the problem
Your thoughts are perversive
You aren't excused

The Queen's Garden

Full of confidence
Vast with beauty

A fine hierarchy of flowers
A satisfactory complexion
A divine court of powers
In each and every section

She knew her body
She knew her mind
Translated she knew her land
One of a kind

Their queen's garden was pure,
A sanctuary for the broken hearted

A Truth

Constant.
We try, we try, we try
But when do we breathe?

Trust is a virtue
You can never rely
On someone's presented nature

Sometimes they are not who we think
Yet we are expected to 'take it'
'Laugh it off'

No.
You are stronger
They need to try;
Evolve themselves to kindness

You Told Me I Couldn't

Question; answer
To and fro
I said; can I?
You told me no

None the wiser
No one else knew
The power over me
I saw through

Once an invisible cage
A mental drain
Freed; I burnt the sage
You were never sane

You said I "couldn't"
But why should that stop me?
You said I couldn't
So I carried on.

Love,
Aimee

5.0

BLACK AND WHITE:

A LANGUAGE

An Introduction To Asperger's

LITERALLY, figuratively
birthed knowingly into the unknown
in the end we stuck together, thick and thin
a connection built on trust; family

LITERALLY, figuratively
defined by an unconscious disadvantage
an emotional shipwreck, splintered throughout
a disconnection built on rarity; Asperger's

LITERALLY, figuratively
to love without fully experiencing
a curious soul struggling from deep within
a constant misfire; potential

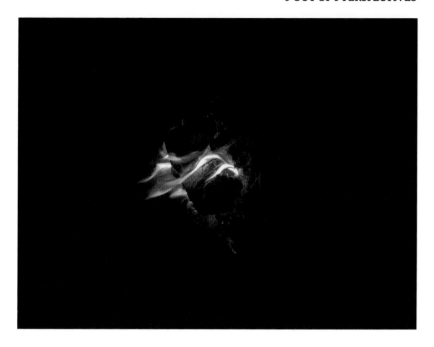

Deep Water, No Swimming

We don't choose to sink,
Life surrounds us
We don't try to over think,
Thoughts consume us

Once you are submerged
There is no 'breathing'
There is no 'fixture'
Only tears and heaving

Once you can feel
It is everlasting
It is internal
Merely shadow casting

Mental health pursues a new life
Do not fall into the tide, swim

A Beautiful Day Outside

It's a beautiful day outside
But have you looked back in?

It's a sky of bright colour
An assortment of light
But what is really going on
Behind our sight?

Late nights spent crying
What if I lose?
Day times spent prying
What if I choose?

Evidently Platonic

There is so much we desire
Yet so little we keep hold
There is so much we admire
Yet so little that stays bold

I want my future
But not waste time away
So I keep grasping at happiness
Little can I say

Just bare with me
I will get there in the end
You will see
My heart WILL mend

Tiger Eye

One word. Astounding

You astound me every single day
By every single hurdle you break away
You will always be my hero

Your core is built upon fire
Your head is made of steel
Your heart is filled with desire
Beauty and kindness is real

I sometimes still worry,
That you won't make it alone
But then I think to myself
And I pick up the phone

Luna – Dedicated To Very Special Lady, Della X

A star
A whirlwind
Not far,
We have walked

The world through your eyes is simplistic,
Through mine it is far from polite
As loyal as can be
You watch through the night

I know there is evil,
I've stared him in the eyes
Once, twice, three times too many
But unknowingly so have you

Luna, pray with me
As we venture through the fields
Thinking to ourselves
What if we had emotional shields?

Luna, hold my hand
With your dainty paw
Telling you my story
You listen in awe

My story...

Survivors come in all shapes and sizes, all forms and emotions, and in all paths of life. Now, I know this is not a terminal illness like cancer, and I do not wish to compare it; but it is still a survival if you make it, and I made it. Sexual assault PTSD is an influence in a lot of young and old peoples lives. It happens to men as well as women, but it is never 'okay'. My story is alike a few others, as BLANK was someone I knew and was in fact in love with, in a long term relationship with; which I thought was built on affection but in turn was fed on manipulation and control. It's not as easy to say "well why didn't you notice the signs " or "why did you let it get that far" because I was the one in love, and love is indeed blind to reason. I finally realised what had been truly happening these past few years, and I was in shock. I had pretended for such a prolonged period of time that it was love, when I was being abused emotionally and physically. It showed me how real this all is.

However, I did not deal with it well at the time. I overdosed and ended up in hospital. I then proceeded to harm myself ending back up in hospital again. It was a vicious cycle of worthlessness because I knew he had taken something I could never get back. I was clinically diagnosed with severe depression and anxiety/OCD. I tried to feel again by dating many 'boys' but it never helped. I was far too damaged and they knew it. Some took advantage of me and I suffered several more assaults. I ended up back in a self destructive cycle. I was on antidepressants, ADHD medicines as well as multiple sleeping drugs. I was trying to stay alive inside the emotional centre of my brain and I genuinely didn't know if I could. But my mum was there every step of the way beside my bed doing for me what I couldn't, and I will never be able to thank her enough because she saved me by proving I could live merely on the basis that there were others who cared for me when BLANK didn't.

I lived for her, with her, day by day. This is when I learnt one of the most important lessons of life; surviving is an achievement. Surviving the day is an achievement, ESPECIALLY on its own, even if it's spent in bed. I now live by this daily through the good and bad times, because they both come and go for eternity, you just have to accept them for what they are, and you for who you are. I accept that I am damaged. I accept that I am now emotionally dependant. I accept that I am different. But I wouldn't have it any other way because there will be someone out there who loves me for exactly those reasons, even if it is only my family. Mum sat beside me as I hyperventilated and cried for hours screaming how I "couldn't do it" and "didn't want to live anymore". You see, because of BLANK I struggle to be alone as my ptsd makes me feel loneliness a whole lot more. It is all very real when there are no forced distractions. The moment when my younger sister Eryn brought me a card saying "Mimi I love you more than anything" and texted me every morning without fail to make sure I was up is what brought me tears of happiness for the first time. It's not easy, but I do it for them, and sometimes I find the strength to do it for me too. My life is constantly up and down with emotions coming and going so I have relapses sometimes, but I'm still here so that means something, and I appreciate every single one of you, even if I don't say it enough.

Sub-note; Even if you choose to keep quiet, It doesn't mean that they got away. I got the chance to show him what he did was real and people cared. I wonder daily how it affects him but I will never know, and I do not need to know. Writing helps me with these thoughts and I think I can now explain candidly in my own way that detachment is possible without noise, just trust yourself.

Mental illness is NEVER something to be ashamed of. People come in all shapes, sizes, colours, weights, and mental forms. Use your experience whether it is a neuro developmental mental illness, one sided by PTSD, ADHD based or even an issue rooted in emotional instability. Living is an achievement, whether some days you just 'live' in bed. If you're struggling, be proud.

Always be kind.

Love,
Aimee xx

Printed in Great Britain
by Amazon